Beyond Dreams

Collection of Thoughts

Anurag Achal

INDIA • SINGAPORE • MALAYSIA

ISBN 979-8-89066-965-0

Dedicated To

My maternal grandmother Chandrika Devi.

My parents, Sindhu Jha and Manoj Kr Jha.

They are my guide, my pathfinders.

My wife Shruti and my children Vinayak and Parth,

My torch-bearers for a fulfilling route.

CONTENTS

EDUCATION AND BOOKS

Education was a motivation yesterday;

Education is a destination today.

Education will be a revolution tomorrow.

Education is a demarcation
Between good and bad
If you know when, where, why
And what to choose, then
You really are educated.

Education: A way to attain

The highest reality.

Education is not about

Knowledge and information

Actually, it's all about the ability

To think and imagine.

Education must not be
Set as an ordinary
Set of goals; it should
Be set as an extraordinary
Set of goals.

Opt for a work which can
Take away your dissatisfaction,
Make you capable and gives
You satisfaction through the
Means of pen and paper.

Teaching is an art;
Studying is a skill.
Where art and skill meet,
The learner breaks his barriers.
And it results in the all-round development
And progress, in leaps and bounds,
Of the learner.

Apply permutation and

Combination to the learner.

Only then can you become

A true teacher.

When you educate
A child, you tend him
To be wise, not to
Be wild.

Education is a foundation,
On which you can build
Your reputation.

A teacher is a generator;
Students, his operator.
Time to time fuel knowledge
With what actually matters.

You can start an opposite
Equation. But always remember,
You are known by your profession.
A teacher should never forget
His position.

A good teacher is a learner's
Pleasure, and a good learner
Is a teacher's treasure.

Education is a tool on which
You sit and make the
Environment cool; and with
Its possession, no one can trap
And make you a fool.

If you are taught,
You ought to know
How and why you write
A thought.

When the earth

Won't give you,

The sky is open.

A thought is a bundle of opinions,
Cast or experienced under
Different circumstances.
Actually, it's a reflection
Of one's own inner self.

The mark of a pen is always
Dark. Once enlightened, be
Ready to embark. Convert
Your writings like a shark;
Deep in side the ocean,
Who can build a park?

When you are lost in
Imagination, you create
Potential thought with
Determination.

It you don't gain knowledge,

Nobody is at your privilege.

I can’t play with my
Teaching profession
Because it’s my entire
Possession.

When you hire knowledge,

You can't fulfill the

Desire of your college.

Education is a voyage

That knows no age.

Board knowledge is

The luggage.

Knowledge is like foliage
With and within the age.
It's never been spoilage.

The sun of education

Never sets. It's always 24x7.

It's a way for heaven. Without it,

There is no reason of freedom.

****

As clip is for hair.
Apply cream to be fair.
Likewise, knowledge
And education are for the chair,
Here and there; actually,
Everywhere.

I am on a multi-purpose

Project. Still, I do well

In my subject.

When you are keen
Enough to be injected
With Knowledge... Oh, my Lord,
Make me infected with
Knowledge.

The thing that we eat
Get rotten, but the things
That we learn shouldn't be
Forgotten.

Whatever is taught,

It’s outcome must

Be a thought.

Education has no
Season. From time
Immemorial till now,
Education is the only reason.

Pick for the peak,

So that you can speak.

Where education is

A number, there everyone

Should surrender.

My mission is not to
Be rich monetarily. I
Still want to enrich my
Vocabulary.

Education is a mirror.
When you see and it reflects,
Your intellect is reflected,
In seconds, minutes, and an hour.

With the advent of
Smart phones, there
Is a little bit of
Engineering in everybody's
Life.

Education is our
Soulmate. Without
It, how can we
trace and chase the
date?

Education is our

Soulmate, with whom we

Are passionate. Even if

Sometimes, we are

Late, we reach to

learn inside our schoolgate.

If you desire
A career, you have
To wait for the carrier.
You ought to go beyond
The barrier.

A teacher is also a learner

Because he has spent

Miles in the corner.

Education is for all; it never gets foul,
With its fragrance, it's like rose petals,
Connected to the soul, education is
For the whole. It Teaches then reaches
For the concerned goals.

It you have a thirst for knowledge,

It ensures that your first village is

An embodiment of an educational cottage.

Learners are like a stream
Which flow. The school ensures
Their throughout glow.

I still

Search for doubt, despite

the fact I have

Taught the chapter throughout.

Education never goes on
Vacation; it's like an everyday
Function. It's a junction
To reach our desired destination.

Convocation of the alumni
Is no less than a ceremony.
Years after years, they are still in harmony.

Education is a joy, but
Unfortunately, everyone
Doesn't enjoy.

The wise are cool, and

The fools desire

To rule.

Learn and read with greed
Because education knows no
Creed. Guru Dron asked
For Eklavya's right thumb and
Killed when the invincible Karan
Was freed.

Life is all about age.

Only he can teach,

Who has the courage.

A teacher is a classic
Actor who defines everyone's
Character.

A thought speaks a lot
For what we have and for
What we have got.

A thought never fails.

Even if it is for years stale.

The rude turns to
Be wise, where knowledge
And education is its price.

I know that you

Are able, but now,

I am capable.

If you are educated,
You remain updated.

Education coming from the
Generation will continue.
For generations, this is the
One and only season.

Education is a set of

Goals by which everyone

Has his/her roles.

Education is a true
Delight. With knowledge
And wisdom, you soar the heights.

Education gradually
Makes you right
When you learn to write.

Education is such
An affair which
Enables a person to
Sit on the chair.

Food and education,
Growth and foundation:
The needs of every nation.

Education is the
Theme of life,
It doesn't matter if
It doesn't rhyme.

The ability to think wisely
And make a judgment is far
Better than having good
Academics or having a better
Higher education.

Educational values that you inherit are
Far more important than the values
That you Cherish.

A person blessed with creative and
Imaginative power can take himself
To the original corridors of power and
Ensure to prove his mettle there.

My debut in the field of
Literature is a proof of
My past victory.

Debit your illness;

Credit your wellness.

Degrees and knowledge don't matter.

In the long run, all that matters is

Your practical approach toward life.

Make study a sort of fun, so that in the Future, it might not turn to be boredom.

Garner the support and love of your
Colleague at work; it is very crucial
For the successful running of an institution
And the harmonious development of the learner.

Keep on teaching and learning so that the
Options that create the learner
Could become a milestone in both lives.

Sound knowledge doesn't make a sound
Teacher; because a teacher is also a
Learner throughout their life.

The pen is one of the cheapest
Things in nature, but it does
the costliest things for
Mankind.

Feeling or thoughts must not be made
To soothe one's mind, but it should
Be directed to soothe one's soul.

Your actual age begins when you
Start learning, irrespective of
The age you are in.

To become a teacher, the biggest
Challenge before you is to ensure
How the best minds should work
In the best directions, thereby fulfilling
The needs of the country.

The pencil is used to write, an
Eraser to erase, a sharpener to
Sharp. The co-ordination of the
Three is instrumental in shaping
The child's basic education.

Your knowledge is your qualification,
Not your degrees, which make a
Difference, either in the beginning
Or in the end.

You can't have superior brains unless
You are blessed, not only by the almighty
But also the blessings of your
Mother and father.

With imagination, everything is
Possible.

Thoughts or thinking, which when given a
True shape, becomes a well-known and
Meaningful script and a major
Source of inspiration for others.

A good imaginative person can be a good

Dreamer, and a good dreamer may be

A good imaginative person.

Textbooks should be made or edited
In such a manner so that the cultural and
Social heritage of the learner should
Be kept intact.

School is the best saviour
Of mankind; the
Basic hub of knowledge
Received and imparted.

The learner and the learned
Are an inseparable part of
The mode of education.

The world is a genuine place for
Competitors: the more marks you
Obtain, the better your chances
Of winning.

Your routine contact and your regular
Visiting of your institution can bring
Laurels for you.

When you write a meaningful script,
It merely coincides or contradicts.
But, that doesn't matter. All that matters is the
Content and practical approach, which becomes
A big affair and is ready for inscription
Worldwide.

Education doesn’t mean to argue with the

Learner but to

Quench the thirst of the of the learner’s argument.

Your ambition shouldn't be your goal,

Your faith should be your goal.

Faith and ambition are

Interdependent on each other.

Generally, reading writing won't work.

You have to try something different

And do something different.

Thought, quotes, and ideas are
In my mind. I have written
It for all of
Mankind.

The chief aim of education is not
Meant to fulfill your basic needs; it's
Aim is to make you extraordinary
Form ordinary.

Writing a script in a true sense
And true spirit should be in such
A way so that it may coincide
With anyone living or dead.

When you become a master of your

Own self, circumstances turn in your favour.

When you observe, then you write.
Because only a good observer can be
A good writer.

Receive your work like a fool,

And perform your work like

A genius.

A visit or a short trip to school is a
Genuine feature in everybody's life.
Its memory resonates in each
And every heart.

Your views are reflected if your
Actions and efforts are up to
The mark.

Physically, you stand;

Mentally, you work.

There is a deep connection

Between the two.

When you start writing
Something beyond your capacity,
And its meaning to yourself is
Not clear, you become a true writer.

A teacher in his lifetime gives millions of
Autographs, which are the most meaningful
And authentic, and thereby, he makes millions
Of lives successful.
The most eligible
Autograph; he is a star in true sense.

When your prime time to build a
Career goes off uselessly, a miracle
Alone can save you, which cannot
Be defined.

Books teach you the art of living if
You are fully engrossed with them. It will
Take you to unthinkable heights.

Human brains and books are inseparable.

If it is separated, the matter of

The concerned fails.

Since time immemorial, books and
Scholars share vibrant bonds,
Which is the only path to success,
Ensuring the simple become scholars.

Knowledge is succeeded by wealth.

Book a book.

It's the only

Reason to eat and cook.

Today is a challenge.

Tomorrow you write.

As a teacher,

You teach what is wrong and what is right.

The books at its might,
When it becomes gradually,
Readers delight.

Literary works are the result of

Talented and imaginative persons.

A man without knowledge is like

A drought-hit place.

Thoughts are all a matter of
Imagination: the more you imagine,
The more you determine, the
More the chances of margin.

Make the learner up to date with

Your creative talents.

He who is blessed becomes a teacher.

Capability doesn't lie physically; it's

All about how strong mentally you are.

If you write a script, and it works,

It means you have hit the target.

A thought is an idea in itself, which,
If implemented, would
Do wonders for the concerned.

Creativity is almost dependent
On imaginations. Only an imaginative
Persons can be more creative.

School-going children are ornamental
In themselves, and the role of the
Teacher is to adorn them with
Knowledge and ensures their brightness.

Pursue for work which soothes
Yours senses, maximises your
Ability, and minimises your
Frustration level and anxiety.

The human mind is like the contents of a
book; it is enlisted on a page or
A memory frame. The idea is
The more you work, the more you get
Out of it.

Human brains and books share a
Healthy relationships between themselves.
Both of them are a double-sided
Affair. They can't work or do things alone.

Books teach you an art of living if you are
Fully engrossed with them. They take you to
Unthinkable heights.

Human brains and books are inseparable. If they
Are separated, the motto of the concerned
Fails.

A book needs a cover,

A teenager needs a lover,

A house needs residents. Moreover,

A sound intellect needs a

Suitable drawer.

When the business is from
Your brain, you have
To mention in your
Book about your pain.

Today, a chef (cook) must
read a book, as well as
Mend his looks.

A book is a toy for the kids.
It gives them joy
And fulfils their needs.

SPIRITUALITY, DIVINITY AND GOD

In India, animals are not
Merely animals; they are divine characters
Who are closely associated with
Different Hindu Gods and Goddess.

I have completed my internship
in divine management today, and I am
Looking forward to a
Better placement.

A saint cursed a man

And said, “Go to hell.”

Very gently, he replied,

“All is well.”

Temples are a place for
Worship; they're also a place
For gossip and interaction with
The almighty. Who can ask,
'Where is Almighty's office?'

Divinity is at its best

When visibility is at

Its rest.

Disappointment is an appointment

With the Almighty.

Inspite of chance, I am not devoid
Of glance; it's a beautiful stance.
Oh, my god, ensure my literary dance; fulfil
All my plans.

What you can see in a fraction of
Seconds, you can't see it in fraction
Of long hours. So connect with almighty
To Add your calculation powers.

Calculate your prayer
With the divine tower. Then,
You will actually realize
Your inner power.

Select your soulmate,

And connect with the

Ultimate.

I have a strong affinity
towards of spiritualism, but
That doesn't mean I don't
Believe in secularism.

When you have a lot of challenges
In your life, look upside down and
Inside out. The Almighty is on
Your side.

Towards divine,
Almighty is mine.
He ensures that everyone shines.
Prayers act as a catalyst and enzyme.
He ensures that everyone shall remain fine.

If you sit under the
Roof with your family,
Remember always, you
Remain with the Almighty happily.

The tinking bells of prayers
That I hear has made me
God's dear.

Your prayers will never go in
Vain; you will realise later,
How and why, when you
Board a plane or a train.

The almighty sets the trends.

We are mere puppet in his hands.

Your waste can also become

An important one in the

Eyes of the Almighty if you are

In His good books.

Trust in supreme power; He will help
You when the whole world discards
You.

Festivities are a great occasion
To celebrate together and seek
Divine blessings from the
Almighty.

It you haven't enjoyed the worldly
Pleasures which are meant to be
Enjoyed, a disaster from which the
Almighty can love and reward you therein.

Invoke the invisible and face him.

To be visible by your hard work and innocence.

Innocence is the most important aspect
Of the spiritual life.

Whatever you achieve,
Credit goes to the Almighty as
He is the guiding force in all forms.

Actually, loving is a way to
Attain divinity if it is pure
And done in a conducive atmosphere.

Seeing the invisible, where success
Stems from, is daunting but
not an impossible task.

It doesn't take much time for a
Person to attain divinity. A quarter
Of a person's life is enough to do so.

Planting and nurturing saplings
is like caring and nurturing
A new born child. Both are God
In different forms.

The mercy of the Almighty is not to

Show but to feel.

If you haven't enjoyed the worldly
Pleasures, Godly pleasures are
Waiting for you.

Small investments are just like offerings and
Prayer to the Almighty. Both of them
Become a major force after along
Time.

Tremendous gain after a lot of
Hardship is possible only after
The blessings of the Almighty.

How hard is it to get
True love. If one has it, he is blessed.

Sense of your belongings should not be
Material; they should be spiritual.

God's approval and mercy are
Necessary for the beginning of
Good things.

God bats for the person if he
Is pure and innocent.

Material gain can be measured,
But spiritual gain cannot be measured.

The ending one's life is not a
Solution for any ills because
An unseen power stands to
Guide us enroute of failures.

God provides power to person in
Different forms.

It you can sacrifice

You will be able to meet the God

Mahadev, who has three eyes.

After seeing the ultimate thing,
One doesn't desire more from
This world.

Empowering oneself with an essence
Of spirituality is a great thing.

Escalating on a traditional, spiritual,
And modern aspect is a clear sign
Of good beginnings which leads to
Just ends.

True success and happiness don't
Depend upon materialistic progress
But the culmination of both
Spiritual and material aspects.

Nothing can match divine
Powers which thereby leads to
Prosperity and happiness.

Once you get a divine connection,

Things start to happen automatically.

Progress is a virtue.
Development is a virtue.
To ensure these virtues happen you have to
Invoke the divine virtues that are
Lying within yourself.

Divinity is not a gift; you have

To earn it.

Once when you become a part of
Divine light, you have nothing
To worry about.

When you are blessed, God understands
Your needs and works accordingly.

When a person sees an ultimate
Donor, he becomes an ultimate
Receiver gradually.

Idols are the symbols or the
Primary stages of Gods and Goddess.
But your worth matters if you
Find or see the originals.

Empowering yourself by eating is not
The formulae. Empower yourself
By devotion towards the Almighty.

Spiritualism and materialism
Complement each other:
Both go hand in hand.

A person become a part of more
Prominent technology which
Exists only after a big spiritual
Progress.

There are seven wonders in the world
Which can be seen by the naked
Eye. But there are still many wonders
Which are unseen, unfelt, and yet
To be explored.

If you are spiritually high, you are
At par with the Almighty.

God alone is the symbol of love,
Who judges people and rewards
Them correctly.

The moment you come to Earth,
You get enrolled in the attendance
Register of the Almighty.

Time is God.

If you can manage time,

You can manage God.

God's blessings can take you to unthinkable Heights.

When you propose to high spiritual
Powers innocently, He is at your disposal;
In both formats: spiritually and
Materially.

Nothing is unconditional on the earth
Or in heaven. Everything has a
Condition; even love.

If you are talking of divinity,
It is not a worldly affair; it's something
Special and powerful whose realisation
Is very difficult.

If you cannot adjust in an unjust and
Inhumane society, the just and divine
Society is awaiting you.

Intentional effort won't fetch you
Divine blessings. Sustained
Efforts with determination unintentional
Paves your way towards heaven.

There are two worlds: the visible
And the invisible. By virtue of birth,
You become the member of this world,
And gradually by virtue of work, you
Become a member of the invisible world.

Miracles happen; wait and hope for them.

You fall under the jurisdiction of the
Almighty when you are mentally
And physically ruined.

Faith in the Almighty is the most
Expensive property accumulated
Gradually in life.

I think I can write more on destiny.
How will things occur? How will things
Happen within the passage of time
And within the passage of my age?

When you handle a candle
Remember, it's Christ and
Church from where were taken
The idea of India's preamble.

A person with values laden
Remains in the Almighty's observation.

The flavour of modernity added with
The taste of spirituality makes
One's life easier and enables us to
Attain great heights and prosperity and
Comes very early in life.

I am at the God's doorstep,

But I

Don't know the way to the staircase.

When God will claim,
You will win lots of acclaim.

God's plan is unanimous.

It's not meagre;

It's more than surplus.

People usually say,

"Oh, my God."

Please tell me,

Who can forget the

Lord?!

God shall prevail,
But tell me, who
Will avail?

SUCCESS AND IDEAS

I have a success story.
But I don’t have a success
History: this marks my victory.

The definition of success is very
Complex as if Counting stars
In the night.

I can claim for my idea, but
I can't blame another's area.

There is a hidden power in ideas which
Comes to the forefront gradually with
Repeated attempts to think and act
Positively.

The certainty of relationships lie
Only and only when a person
Becomes successful.

Ideas become a part of a person's
Life when one's mental ability
Rises beyond recognition, which
Thereby marks the making of a legend.

A period when your expectation
Grows ideas bloom and love talks
Is a period of culmination which
Changes you from the inside out.

Success earned is more

Important because

You can't inherit success.

Ideas converted into technology

Be it an invention of a Plane or the steam engine.

They are actually inventions.

Thoughts, quotes, and ideas
Are in my mind. I have written
Them for the all of mankind.

An idea when adjusted makes

The person wise and just.

When you proceed, then you succeed.

When success knocks at your

Door, you must dance on the floor.

When ideas turn to money,

Then there is no question of price.

When you have a target of miles,

Then only you can compile.

When an idea is searched, it is a most

Sought after affair.

Your complete transformation

Is ensured after a series

Of setbacks on your way towards

Success.

A good entrepreneur has a clear map
Of roadblocks in his vision and makes
His venture a successful one by
Acting accordingly.

Your ideas become a source of
Inspiration for others when it has
Potential intensity.

Success in one field is a trend which tends

For the failure in other.

You never know how and when
Ideas would come and empower
And enlighten your way.

When you become successful, people
Follow you. But when you're unsuccessful
People discard you.

The extent of your mass appeal alone

Defines your professional success.

An invention is an idea.

Success comes to those who obeys

The rules.

Wonderful and excellent ideas
Should be reflected through a script
So that world knows it, and it generates
Powerful scientific technology.

Technology: An idea in the primary Stage.

Your match with a superior one in

Itself is a powerful idea.

Ideas can make you large if it is

Up to the mark.

It you are brimming will new and
Innovative ideas the world is at your feet.

Ideas generate when you

Co-operate.

When you collide with success again
And again you coincide with
Ideas that you gain.

When you blink your eyes,

Success gets you twice because

Mahadev has three eyes

Father of all the wise.

Success requires constant

Practice; then ideas

Come in with tactics.

Mahadav is the destroyer;

He is my ideas provider.

I am not the author of the book.

His is on my side with his divine favour.

The book has many flavors.

Success has no terms and conditions;
You be satisfied with a single
Idea. It will take you to
Your desired destination.

Success will take you to the top.

Thereafter, your ideas

Can’t stop.

If you believe you are completely
Successful, you are at
The doorstep of success.

Success never goes in vain;

It results in the ideas

That are main.

Your ignorance sometimes can

Become your secret to success.

If success would have been
Permanent, there would have
Been no temperament.

Success is like creation; it

Requires a lot of dedication.

Success is about chance;
Success is about dance.
Success is all about laughter, jokes
And romance.

Basking in the warmth of success

Won't work, attempt for the

Next one.

DREAMS, DESITNY, MYSTERY, AND MEDICAL SCIENCE

Dreams are therefore that is when you lay.

It doesn't cost anything, No one can pay.

Dreams are an indication which decides your past, present, and future condition.

Dreams are a wonderful way.
Everyone has a story to say.
Dreams empower us in the night
Which shapes our day.

Dreams excess;
You will find access.
The dreams will lead you
To beyond success.

Believe me, dreams too are fair,

When you don't compare.

Dreams will take you to the top,

But when you awake get ready for your job.

Dare to dream

Rarely it means a

Proper cure is

Its theme.

A dream is a display on the subconscious mind,

When the consciousness comes in, we play in the ground,

Beyond both everything is found;

Beyond dreams everything is profound.

Dreams are a spirit
Where we split
Then we meet
No one knows why, how
And whom to greet.

Believe me, dreams too are fair,

When you don't compare.

Dreams will take you to the top,

But when you awake get ready for your job.

I have never even dreamt of writing a book but please read the contents

I suppose you are content with it.

A dream is a fusion of the body and the mind available to the mankind.

Dreams are like creepers,
The more they creep,
The less one sleeps.
Still the body and mind are at peace.

You can't mend your destiny with your money if you bend spiritually;

It's your divine journey.

Destiny is not known where the history is to reckon.

One has nothing to do, Destiny takes its own course followed by hard work and honesty.

Dreaming and achieving are the two sides of the same coin,

Both are essential ingredient of each other.

Destiny changes for a person every.

Now and then, it depends upon the

Means adopted to fulfill the

Purpose.

The dream that you dream
Is a dream until it turns into
Reality. That is called success in
One and another way.

The brain is the most complicated
Form of technology whose functions
Are still a mystery for the scientists.

The moment you dream, you are
In the eternal world.

Dream and imagination are part of
Each other. Both compliment each
Other.

My dreams are my mirror of my
Unknown, untold unseen world.

The wonderful things that can’t be
Seen but it can be converted into
A virtual reality only through dreams.

Dream, dream, dream.

Your success resides

Therein

Complications come to a heal and

Recover the body and soul.

Then are many technologies existing in the
World and is very real yet it is
Beyond the reach of mankind and
Medical science.

The more beautiful your imagination

The most beautiful your dreams.

Dreams comes at par with reality

With only a few trend-setters.

Observe it.

A Mystery is the most awaited
Thing with its input and output.

A life can become part and parcel
Of destiny if you make yourself,
A part and parcel of Mystery.

A mystery awaited is a mystery

Solved.

If your sleeping is guided by a

Force can do miracles for you.

When you can see the future, you

Can define the present aptly.

When you are in search, you need
A torch but before a fraction of
Seconds brightness is ensured which is
A part and parcel of diving hide
And seek affair.

You can't be cured by the medical
Sciences unless your prayers are
Heard by the ultimate sciences which
Is unseen, untold, and unfelt.

Doctors prescribe, but

Who subscribes?

The breakthrough in medical science is at
Par with the invisible science, where
Both works a miracle is expected.

Invisible science is more

Powerful than the modern science.

What and how human brain has
Developed is a matter of mystery,
And thereby search for the medical
Science.

The possibility of solution of a problem
Doesn't lie in according to it but in
Detaching it and diagnosing it immediately.

The history of mystery

Is unknown.

When you mix chemistry
With mystery, it's also like
an unknown treasury.

Mystery is hungry for
mystery, whose appetite
can't be understood by everyone.

Where we come from,

Where we go;

This is a mystery nobody

Knows.

Mystery is a mystery
Because there is no
Discovery of mystery

Enjoy sick,

Someone will pick.

This is the trick,

Where medical science

Comes at risk.

LOVE AND ROMACE

The sperm is a germ.
But when it fertilizes,
It makes the world run.

It doesn't matter

How is now your GF

At the end of the day, all

That matters is what is your PF.

Crown on the head and
Gown on the body, the
Space lefts knows everybody

Put your mind and make
Your work so strong that
You may have an affair
With the Almighty.

I haven't proposed,
But I suppose it doesn't
Matter whether
It's open or close

If you are on a date,

Obviously you have to

Relish on dates.

Grace has to do everything
With the face because
You romance on the earth
Not in space.

At the Cost of me

Price is for the fiancé.

The efficacy of size

Defines the beauty

Inside.

You rely to fly

But near about is

Never a lie.

I am in a sort of fun
Today as I have been
Embedded by a gem.

When you love with
Your heart and soul
He/she will take you
To the desired goal.

In and out

Romance is a

True delight.

In love with your
Partner after getting
The approval of society
Through the institution
Of marriage is a general
Phenomenon.

The most important thing
That one should seek in ones
Partner is character of life.

Initially the things that

Are small gradually

Become large.

The trends are
Visible earlier, but
The harvest is
Done a little later.

Relationships are a token of love,
Between the lover and the beloved, where
The eternal bond is never broken.

PANDEMIC

The pandemic was treacherous
And deadly which the mankind
Faced boldly

Pandemic taught us a lesson
Which removed everybody's illusion

When pandemic was at its prime

One and all decline, nobody

Claimed it was mine

no knock on the door
Corona was a block on the floor

Pandemic gave us sufferings
Anxiety stress and worry there
Was no place for so sorry this
Is the pandemic's entire story

Pandemic was a ghost which is now
Lost, killed and destroyed the
World uniformly the deadlier
Most every now effects are there
Pre or post

Corona will be bitterly remembered
When we look back at the
Memories in the calendar.

Pandemic was an ugly face in the
Mirror which showed its terror.
Needless to say, it was an ultimate
Horror.

Corona warriors were those

Who lost their lives for a

Noble cause.

FOOD, HUNGER, MALNUTRITION, POVERTY, AND POPULATION

Oh! my diety.
Convent poverty into
Property. It ensures
Each and everyone's
Prosperity, whether its
Village, town, or city.

How better it would be
For the world to make
Poverty an endangered species.
But there are only debates
And lofty speeches.

Poverty-ridden world. All of a
Sudden it will fall. Oh, my Lord!
Turn my this Wish so that everyone
Gets a hot soup in a bowl.

Drink water to heal

Don't always relish

On sumptuous meal.

The devotee of Krishna is always ready.
The entire world knows how shabby
Sudama was turned wealthy. A victim
Of poverty, malnutrition, hunger, and food.

You will fade without food, but the
of trees in autumn are its ample proof.

When the food is limited, there is the presence of

Love as we share among ourselves, whereas in abundance

of food, there is a lasting as it goes carefree.

Food has a role to play, look
At the veg roll; it's on display.

Who lives in poverty?

Ask him what is his property.

Money will teach you a lesson
Which will define your kitchen

When poverty will be in danger,

nobody will remain hunger.

Population is not a pollution,
It's manpower from generation
To generation who decide the
Resources optimal utilization.

Compromise is not a

Solution. India now has

The world's largest population

You can eliminate hunger,

But how can you stop malnourishment?

Poverty is a very big punishment.

Child and children this is a
Mathematical differentiation

A little bit of salt without which
All the aroma and taste will
Come to halt.

NATURE

We are mortal

Nature is immortal

No summary no conclusion

This story is obviously total.

Nature inspires.
Many come, many expires.
Sometimes ice, sometimes it's fire;
Nature in itself is a beautiful sattire.

Nights are fulfilled,

Days are fulfilled.

Nature never stops

To yield.

Can I talk with the tree?

Yes, they say I am

Always free.

A courtyard without trees
Is like a vehicle without grease.

My father has gone out of the farm,
Wherein lies the Indian villages.
Charm till now, with his old arms.
He has done no harm, my most
Adorable, my best gram.

In the lap of nature, I am
Sitting on the furniture.
Isn't it an ironical gesture.

Flow of water;

Flow of current

This issue is very urgent. All that

Matters is who is the agent.

Flowers bloom and shed.
One day likewise everyone
Will be decayed.

Nature is a torch-bearer,
Where there is a lot of pressure.
After that, it is a mesmerizing
Pleasure.

GAMES, SPORTS, AND IPL

The Indian premier league

Is a very big leap for

The cricketers. Who keeps

And upkeeps them? Does it matter?

The cricketers are know by their clean sweep.

IPL is a game, where
Name, fame, and wealth
Remain the same. A game of uncertainty
Can unite. All are gifted men.

Games and sports define a person's
Identification. Their ability to play,
Which display their team spirit and
Leadership qualities.

I believe in progress as a sprinter:
Believe in race, wear your dress,
clean your face, and march forward
With pace.

Easier it was fifty, now it's twenty.

Reduced format introduced,

More vigor and vitality,

In cricket.

Winning the test match will prevail,

I will talk about it later in detail

The format of T20 is designed
In such a way that there is
No match where usual chat is a
Often say.

When you represent your country
In the Olympics, and you seek to be
At the peak, your medal and trophy,
If you win, will alone determine
Whether you are strong or weak.

Nobody can even think
Of BPL when the
Match is IPL.

With cheer girls, there is added
Charm in the 20-20 game. How can
You forget it. It's not mere harm
In its name.

When you win, play;

You are on display.

If you win definitely,

Celebrations will be collectively.

A man requires a fan.
When it is hot, a fan
Requires a particular celebrity
Brand, even if the product is a ban.

T20, I am above forty. I will watch
IPL till I am sixty. Charm will still
Remain till I am eighty. Generation
After generation, friends every time;
It will be 20-20.

If you win a game, it's a matter of
Fame, but if you loose it, it's not a
Matter of shame. Try again. The world
Is full of inspiration. Everyone cares
Who went and who came.

May be you are treacherous, but
Always remember IPL is very glamorous.
“Love it feel it try it,” the world says.
It’s different and fabulous.

The word of IPL

Is the love whom

We select.

IPL is a success story
But it have
A success history; this
Marks the cricketers' victory.

Both a cricketer or footballer

Are defined by their

Supporters.

Where there is smile is on the face,

There beauty is in the race.

Finishing point is the target

Almost in every case.

TECHNOLOGY

No technology can make you competent
Unless you are rooted in your basics.
Where should I hide when the
E-technology is worldwide?

A gadget is an asset which is included in
Everyone's budget.

Shorts are the new e-technology,
Formerly address, now an e-address.

Cut, copy, paste.

E-technology can never

Go waste.

When you delete the memory, you
Make a summary, neither
Permanent nor temporary. In
This process, you create a history.

When you use Wi-Fi,

There is no question of why.

POLITICS

Politics is a game of numbers.
Not for mathematicians but artists
With an ease to achieve the desired
Number (272) by their sheer oratory.
When potential rivals meet and
Agree in a point of public welfare, that
Makes the progress of a leaders.

A corruption-free society can be
Achieved by laying stress on the
Solid foundation of education
Among the young and children.

Sympathetic supporters, critics,
Well-wishers, and followers are a
Few important aspects on which the
Survival of a politician depends.

A politician turns into a statesman
By his ideology of global brotherhood,
International peace, and prosperity
Of the entire world.

The definition of authority is so simple
Power rules in, power rules out: this is the
Connection between powers.

Imitation ensures power for a single

Person, but the theory and practical

Remains undefined.

The abc of politics is more

Difficult then its xyz.

To learn the art of politics is
One thing and to do politics is
Another thing: both follow
Each other.

The crowd-pullers are loved and

Admired by all.

In politics, you never know
Where you can go. So being a
Politician, you obviously you have to
Conduct a road show.

MISCELLANEOUS

A mother can hear because
She has the capacity to bear.

Pay respect to women as they share
A vibrant bond with you by being.
Mother, sister, daughter, and wife.

What would have happened if Pandora
Hadn't opened the box. The Earth
would have turned into heaven,
and the desire for heaven and the
Almighty wouldn't have existed.

My friends,
Don't erode anyone's
Base. Because if not you,
Your next generation will
Come under the case.

Waste also has taste.
Look at the dog licking
At the gate.

Tide comes and goes on

The shore.

Mend your

Side before.

The fruits are in my sight;
I shall eat them with delight.

It you are shy,

Then where is the

Question of why.

If you want to roam,
Book a fight ticket for Rome.
You will find comfort and peace
As if you're in your own home

The amount that you earn,
Where the expenditure is,
Is your turn. This is the
Entire zest of the income that
You must learn.

The grapes are sour,
But now it is not the
Need of the hour.

If you can fulfil your
Promise, it's so nice.
The process decides that
You are wise.

Overcome the obstacles
On your way, and you will
Win a million hearts.

Effective moves at the right
Time ensures one's progress.

Honesty up to the desired level
Is appreciated, exceeding which
May result in the failure of the
Concerned institution or government machinery.

www.ingramcontent.com/pod-product-compliance
Lightning Source LLC
LaVergne TN
LVHW041138150826
845673LV00001B/31
9798890669650